# RUGBY SKILLS

## GARETH EDWARDS
## WITH IAN ROBERTSON

**STANLEY PAUL, LONDON**

# ACKNOWLEDGMENTS

I should like to thank Ian Robertson for all his help in the preparation of this book, Barry John for giving up a day on the golf course to join me for the photographic sessions at the Bank of England rugby ground, and Colin Elsey of Colorsport, who took such excellent photos.

Stanley Paul & Co. Ltd
3 Fitzroy Square, London W1P 6JD

An imprint of the Hutchinson Publishing Group

London Melbourne Sydney Auckland
Wellington Johannesburg and agencies
throughout the world

First published 1979

© Gareth Edwards 1979

Set in VIP Univers Light by
Input Typesetting Ltd

Printed in Great Britain by McCorquodale (Newton) Ltd.,
Newton-le-Willows, Lancashire.

ISBN 0 09 140010 4 cased
      0 09 140011 2 paper

# CONTENTS

# INTRODUCTION

When I retired from international rugby at the end of the 1978 season, I was able to look back on twelve very happy years in which I played rugby all over the world and had the opportunity to examine the contrasting styles and techniques used by the leading players in different countries.

Although there are undoubtedly slight variations in the overall approach to rugby in New Zealand, France, Argentina, Japan and in Britain, I am absolutely convinced that the same basic skills apply everywhere.

Whilst all the great players have their own individual style in everything they do on the rugby field, their basic technique doesn't vary.

It is generally agreed that the game has changed and developed quite a lot during the past decade, but a practical knowledge of these fundamental skills is just as important as ever. Not everything I did on a rugby pitch was a perfect text-book demonstration, but it was pretty effective and it was always based on a sound technique. I have always believed in flexibility and I often improvised until I found a compromise that particularly suited me. The top golfers don't all have an identical swing or hit the ball in exactly the same way, but they do all base their style on a few very important principles. Rugby is just the same.

In this book I try to show how I have developed all the game's basic skills over the years and I hope all the crucial factors are clearly explained and illustrated. Every player, forward and back alike, should be able to pass, catch, kick and tackle and I know only too well that, although I was often described as a natural games-player, it took me twelve long hard years of graft and practice to reach the standard I attained by the end of my career.

I was far from perfect, but I had a decent repertoire of the basic skills that only came from hundreds of hours of dedicated practice. There is no easy way.

Watching golf, tennis or snooker on television, the top players make it all look very easy, but you can be sure that what you are admiring is the end product of endless practice.

Whatever standard you reach, rugby should always be fun. And one thing is certain – the greater command you have of the basic skills, the better you will be and the more fun you will have playing rugby.

*Gareth Edwards, top Welsh try-scorer of all time, making a typical break for Wales against Ireland*

# 1 SCRUM-HALF PASSING

I am not beginning this book with the scrum-half pass because I think it is the most important basic skill, but simply because I have spent most of the past twenty years of my life trying to develop and perfect the art.

Strangely enough, although I have always been a pretty natural athlete, the trademark of every good scrum-half nowadays – the spin pass – was not something I acquired easily.

I spent most of my schoolboy career as a scrum-half dive-passing – the standard method of passing used by all scrum-halves in British rugby in the mid 1960s. As a young kid I simply accepted it and tried to be as good at it as I possibly could.

This early training wasn't a waste of time: I did learn the crucial importance of the scrum-half's bread-and-butter job – to pass as quickly, as accurately and as far as possible. From a very early age I learned that accuracy was the prime essential, and the speed of the pass was much more important than the length. The beauty of the spin pass is that it makes it easy to combine length and accuracy. Speed comes with hours and hours of practice – getting hands and legs in the right position for a quick pass.

I was first conscious of the spin pass when I saw it being used by Ken Catchpole of Australia and Chris Laidlaw of New Zealand. They were two of the best scrum-halves I ever played against and, as early as 1966, they had begun the scrum-half revolution by using the spin pass with dramatic effect.

When I won my first cap for Wales against France in 1967, I had just begun to experiment with the spin pass, but I did not have enough confidence and control to use it during the intense pressures of international rugby.

However, by the time I went with the British Lions to South Africa in 1968, I had decided that it was vital to learn the art of the spin pass. I worked hard at it in South Africa practising every day for three months. By the time I returned to Wales I had mastered a skill which was to stand me in good stead throughout my career.

One of the great regrets I have, looking back, is that I have never learned to spin-pass with my left hand to the same standard I reached with my right hand. I would advise every young scrum-half to try to pass equally well both ways.

In the sequence on the following page I show the technique I use to pass to my left. As you can see, it is one continuous movement from the moment my hands touch the ball until the moment I release the ball. You should avoid picking the ball up from between your legs, as then you need a big backswing to throw a pass more than a few yards.

Ideally the pass should not be lobbed, but the ball should be fired straight at the fly-half in a uniform trajectory like a bullet from a gun. It is also important not to over-reach yourself when you pass – never try to pass further than you can comfortably manage.

The first photo in the sequence (2/1) shows how important it is to position the feet correctly. Whether I am waiting for the ball from the loose, a scrum or a line-out I make sure my feet, and consequently my hands and body, are positioned so that I can dispatch the ball in one continuous flowing movement. As the ball appears from the scrum here, my right foot is beside the ball and my hands are ready to pick

*A great action sequence which shows Gareth Edwards dive-passing from a scrum for Wales against England at Twickenham in 1974*

2/1          2/2

up the ball the exact moment it comes out of the scrum. My head is directly over the ball and my eyes are fixed on the ball. Initially, all my weight is on my right foot. I'm all tucked up ready to uncoil like a spring and unleash the pass.

Everything must be synchronized smoothly.

The moment I pick up the ball I begin to transfer my weight on to my left leg. At the same time I start to rotate my hips, head, eyes and shoulders towards the receiver (2/2). My weight here is more or less evenly distributed with my legs forming a wide base to give the momentum the pass needs.

As I prepare to unleash the pass (2/3) my weight is now on my left leg. I now transfer the momentum and power through my legs and hips so that the final impetus comes from my shoulders, arms and, to a lesser extent, wrists. But, for me, the initial surge of power comes from the legs and hips.

The moment of delivery (2/4) shows that the left hand is used to guide the ball whilst the right hand provides the power and the spinning action. The hands cross to give the spinning action. In picking up the ball (2/1 and 2/2) my right hand is underneath and slightly at the side

of the ball and, to spin-pass, that right hand turns over as it propels the ball towards the receiver.

The left hand is important to guide the ball accurately.

Some scrum-halves don't use their legs fully in spin-passing, but I have always felt the legs are just as important as the shoulders and arms to secure a really long pass. Ken Catchpole used a sharp wrist action with little movement of the arms and shoulders and very little power was transmitted through his legs. He gave an incredibly fast service but it was never a long pass. Sid Going also used his wrists a lot as he whipped the ball away.

But Chris Laidlaw was very much the same as me. His momentum also came at first from his legs and hips. I have always felt this was the best way, because usually legs and hips are stronger and generate more power than shoulders, arms and wrists.

Ideally it is a combination of upper-body strength and agility, combined with the strength from one's legs and hips. That is how I have always passed, but each person must use the method which he finds most comfortable and most effective.

Jerome Galleon is typical of French scrum-halves in that he uses his upper body much more than his legs.

Brynmor Williams and Terry Holmes both use a style similar to mine but, remembering that speed is of paramount importance, they both still occasionally take a step before delivering the pass. That is fatal.

The only way to improve is by practice. There is no simple alternative. The spin pass takes a long time to master. Although I was able to spin-pass in 1968, I still worked at it all through my career to the day I retired, always trying to improve. I strove to make it a fraction faster, a

3/1

3/3

shade longer, even more accurate, every season I played – every year I tried to make my pass a little bit better.

This sequence illustrates something I did a few thousand times between 1967 and 1972 – pass to my great friend and half-back partner Barry John.

Here I follow all the instructions in the first sequence, but it is taken from a slightly different angle and may help to give you another view of the spin pass.

It is worth noting the role of the receiver. Barry has his hands ready to take the ball the whole time. He doesn't begin to move forward until my hands are on the ball. He is motionless in (3/1 and 3/2). That is very important or the

whole three-quarter line will be too flat by the time Barry catches the ball. The fly-half should not creep an inch forward until the scrum-half has the ball in his hands. As I pass (3/3) I am looking at Barry as he begins to move.

He catches the ball cleanly in his hands and not against his chest, so he can quickly transfer the ball to his centre.

The communication between half-backs is obviously important. With Barry and Phil Bennett we started by using verbal codes, often speaking to each other in Welsh during internationals! Other half-backs use hand or foot signals – how you communicate doesn't really matter as long as you both know exactly what is happening.

4/1

4/3

# THE DIVE PASS

The dive pass is used regularly by scrum-halves when, for one reason or another, it is not practical to send out a spin pass. I can think of plenty of situations where the dive pass is the quickest method of getting the ball to the fly-half. If my forwards are being pushed back at a set-scrum and I'm under great pressure from my opposite number and I'm not dealing with good channelled ball, then I usually resort to a dive pass. Similarly, if the ball is tapped wildly out of a line-out away from my reach, I may find it quicker to dive-pass than to get in a position to spin-pass. The same goes for a ball suddenly appearing unexpectedly in the loose. And I have also found the dive pass very useful in dealing with a wet ball.

All the basic rules apply for a dive pass – speed, accuracy and, to a lesser extent, length

are all essential.

Here I approach the ball ready to pass off one foot and never off both feet (4/1 and 4/2). You lose a lot of impetus if you try to pass off both feet. In this case (4/1) my left foot arrives at the ball first, so I prepare to drive off that leg into the pass. It doesn't matter which leg you pass off – it just depends which leg naturally arrives at the ball first. Eyes are kept on the ball until my hands pick it up and I'm all tucked up ready to uncoil (4/2).

As my hands pick up the ball and Barry begins to move, I start to uncoil by driving my left leg hard into the ground as my head turns towards the receiver.

With my eyes fixed on Barry I whip my hands through in an arc as my body drives forwards (4/3), then I break my fall with my hands (4/4), and I'm ready to leap back on to my feet so that I can quickly support my three-quarters. It is worth mentioning again that Barry catches the ball in two hands ready to give a quick pass.

5/1

5/3

## THE REVERSE PASS

The reverse pass is a very useful weapon in every scrum-half's armoury. Even though it is the most difficult pass to master, it can also be the most rewarding. I shall always remember feeding Phil Bennett with a reverse pass in the third test against South Africa in Port Elizabeth in 1974. The pass sent the entire Springbok side the wrong way and left Phil time and room to drop a goal. Mind you, I can also recall all too clearly aiming a reverse pass at Phil Bennett on our own ten-yard line against Ireland in 1975 when we were leading 32-nil. Willie Duggan intercepted it and ran forty yards to score!

As with all scrum-half passing, feet position and balance are important. In the reverse pass, life is complicated by the fact that the scrum-half's momentum is going in the opposite direction to the receiver. This means that for this particular pass, the shoulders and arms play a more significant role in providing the power

than the legs and hips.

With balance so crucial, you should try, if possible, to be reasonably still as you give the pass.

Usually a reverse pass is given under severe pressure when something has gone wrong and you have to whip out a pass quickly whilst facing the wrong direction.

Just like the dive pass, the reverse pass is delivered off one foot from a wide stance. To pass right I approach the ball so my right foot lands beside the ball (5/1). As my hands pick up the ball (5/2) my head begins to turn towards Barry. Although I've played with Barry for years I still look to see where he is, just before passing. This is a difficult pass at the best of times and with my back to the opposition I want to make sure no opposition back-row are in the firing line (Duggan!). With my eyes firmly on Barry, I am ready to release the ball (5/3). The power comes from both hands in this pass as they sweep across my body.

The impetus comes from the arms, the shoulders and a full follow-through (5/4).

15

# PASSING, CATCHING AND HANDLING

Ideally the game is all about running, passing, making breaks, and in the end scoring tries. I have been very lucky throughout my career that the sides I played for – Cardiff, Wales, the British Lions, and the Barbarians – all excelled in adventurous, open rugby. I honestly don't think I would have lasted twelve years at the highest level if I hadn't really enjoyed the fifty or sixty games I played every year. And if I'd been involved in tight nine-man rugby I wouldn't have enjoyed it nearly so much.

Of course, I was very lucky to play at the same time as so many great backs in the Welsh side – Phil Bennett, J. P. R. Williams, J. J. Williams, Gerald Davies, John Dawes and all the others. For the Lions and the Barbarians I had the pleasure to play with Mike Gibson, Tom Kiernan, Andy Irvine, Ian McGeechan, Dave Duckham and Bob Hiller, to name just a few. It was exhilarating to be surrounded by so many brilliant players and I must say I find it all a little sad that the great individual stars seem to have been swallowed up in the last couple of years by the sort of group therapy which the long list of set moves has drilled into every back division – at club and even national level.

Back play has all become very predictable, and international rugby is crying out for a sprinkling of great individual players who are capable of turning a game on their own.

As part and parcel of the squad system I

reckon more players without all the basic skills are reaching higher levels than ever before; we've been confronted recently with centres playing for England who can't even pass properly, let alone make a break.

To rectify the position it is essential for youngsters to learn to pass quickly and accurately, to give and take a pass in one movement, to be able to draw a man in a two-against-one situation, to side-step, swerve, sell a dummy - in short for youngsters to read a situation and be capable of beating a man.

The very first essential must be the ability to give and take a pass, and I must say I'm staggered how many players, backs and forwards, at club and even national level are deficient in this area.

Although passing looks very simple and straightforward when you watch Mike Gibson, Barry John, Dave Duckham or Ian McGeechan giving or receiving the ball, it is in fact one of the most difficult skills to learn. Few youngsters find the orthodox pass completely natural and it does require a lot of practice. Balance is obviously important and a smooth flowing action helps timing and accuracy. But for Peter Squires or J. J. Williams out on the wing and for the likes of Andy Irvine bursting into the line from full-back, speed is essential.

The quick pass will only come after months of practice, and you should begin by making sure your technique is good. With a sound technique you can develop speed, accuracy, and length later.

It always makes sense to run with the ball in two hands, and therefore it makes sense to receive a pass in two hands. If, as many players do, you catch the ball by hugging it in to your chest, it then takes precious moments for you to transfer the ball into two hands ready to pass

Top: *the most-capped international rugby player in the world, Ireland and British Lion three-quarter Mike Gibson, passes to his left to Alastair McKibbon in the Ireland–France match of 1977.* Below: *another outstanding passer of the ball, England's Dave Duckham, falls away after passing to his right during the 1973 England–Wales match*

it on. I always compare this to catching a cricket ball. If someone throws a cricket ball to you, you catch it in both hands in front of you. You do not hug it into your chest. It should be exactly the same with a rugby ball.

As the ball is being passed to me I keep my eyes firmly on it. The moment I have it safely in my hands I look round towards the person I am going to pass to, and briefly, during this split second, I can glance at the opposition defence. Simultaneously, I decide exactly when I'm going to deliver my pass and I know instantly the angle I must pursue to commit my opponent totally (7/1).

As I prepare to pass, my eyes are fixed just in front of the receiver because I want to pass in front of him, so that he can run on to the ball, and not straight at his stomach which will force

him to check his stride before he can take the ball and pass it on to the next player (7/2).

Here I am greatly helped by Barry John because he is holding his hands ready for the pass and so giving me a tangible target to aim at. Looking at his hands, I pass to my left, with my weight on my right leg at the moment I deliver the pass (7/3).

As my hands follow through across my body, my left leg naturally crosses in front of my right leg as my whole body checks and falls away after I release the ball. This hip pass gives the ball momentum and accuracy and has the added advantage of committing my opponent (7/4). If he went straight for Barry before I passed then I could sell a dummy. Note that Barry catches the ball in both hands ready to whip it on.

19

8/1

8/3

The pass to the right is similar. Barry runs with the ball in both hands and the moment he is about to pass he looks round towards me. I have my hands ready to receive the ball in front of me (8/1 and 8/2).

Passing to his right, Barry is balanced on his left leg as he actually delivers the pass (8/3). His right leg crosses in front of his left as he falls away naturally after passing the ball, and I catch the ball in both hands (8/4).

It is worth spending a lot of time practising your passing. You should try and learn to pass

equally well to your right as to your left. Although most players find it easier to pass to the left, the action is exactly the same, so passing to the right should not present any insurmountable difficulty. And without mentioning any names, there are an awful lot of forwards, and a few backs too, that I wish had spent far more time at training sessions running up and down the field improving their passing, and a lot less time taking place-kicks and drop-kicks at goal! For every drop-goal a forward gets in his career, I bet he gives a hundred bad passes and drops a hundred good ones!

21

# QUICK PASSING

Once you've got the basic technique, the next step is to improve the speed with which you can give and take a pass. The very best players can catch and transfer the ball in one movement, giving a fast, long, accurate pass, even under great pressure. To do this it is necessary to catch the ball early and in one flowing movement sweep it across your body and on to the next player. This is the hallmark of a natural ball player and can make a tremendous difference in the time it takes for the ball to reach the wing from the fly-half. The moment I release the ball in this sequence Barry has his hands ready to take the pass. The ball must be passed in front of the receiver or crucial time will be lost (9/1). Barry catches the ball in two hands: his hands are actually reaching out towards me so that he can make contact with the ball as early as possible (9/2). No sooner has he caught the ball than in the very same movement he sweeps it across his body to deliver his pass to Ian Robertson in one continuous action. The moment he catches the ball his head turns towards the person to whom he is passing (9/3).

At the same time, Barry straightens up as he passes, falling away to commit the opposition defence. If he runs towards Ian as he passes and continues in that direction, then his opposite number and the whole opposition cover defence will simply sweep across the pitch in pursuit, completely negating any overlap or break which may be engineered. By straightening the line as you pass, you check the whole opposition defence and this is very important. It means they can't charge across the field in cover defence, in case you sell a dummy or side-step inside. By checking the cover, you give more room to your outside three-quarters and particularly help the running full-back. If you can learn to pass as quickly and accurately as Barry has here, there will also be more room and time for the outside centre, running full-back and wing to operate.

9/3

9/4

10/1

10/2

# CATCHING

Every player ought to be able to catch a kick ahead, although the full-back is probably more involved in this particular aspect of the game than any other individual. But any member of the forwards might be required to catch the ball from an opposition kick-off or during general loose play.

It is essential to keep your eyes on the ball the whole time it is in the air. Once you are confident that you are standing in exactly the right place to catch the ball, you can brace yourself by standing with your legs about shoulder

width apart (10/1). This gives you a solid base in case half the opposition is bearing down to tackle you the moment the ball arrives.

Once the ball is only a few yards away, you should cradle your arms with your fingers pointing towards the sky and prepare to take the catch (10/2).

Eyes still glued to the ball, you should hug it into your chest or stomach as it lands and hold firmly on to it. Just as you catch the ball it is worth turning side-on to the opposition as in 10/3 and 10/4. There are two reasons for this. Firstly, if you are about to be tackled then you can offer a pretty solid hip to absorb the blow, and with your elbows neatly tucked in to your side, the tackler is far more likely to be hurt than you are. Secondly, even if the opposition

24

10/3

10/4

is not within range, if you happened to drop the ball in this position it would not be a knock-on. There would probably be time to recover, pick the ball up and clear any danger.

Along with so many other skills, catching can best be learned in simple stages.

You can practise with a partner and begin by kicking the ball to each other, standing only fifteen yards apart and kicking the ball only a few feet into the air. Confidence will quickly be developed and then it is time to extend both the length and the height of the kicks. As long as both players are catching 90 per cent of the kicks then the length and height can be increased accordingly.

Once you are confident of your ability to deal with the kick ahead, it is time to practise under

pressure. As the ball is hoisted into the air, two or three players should follow up to put you under pressure. But if you are in position, well balanced, with your eyes glued to the ball the whole time and hug it in to your body, you should never have any trouble.

I've been fortunate to have played my whole international career with the best and safest catcher of the ball in the world – J. P. R. Williams. With the whole New Zealand pack charging at him and about to land on top of him, he has never once flinched, taken his eyes off the ball even for a split second or failed to follow all the basic rules. I honestly cannot remember him ever dropping the ball and that has given fifty Welsh sides tremendous confidence during the last twelve years.

11/1

# PICKING UP A ROLLING BALL

Finally in this chapter I think it is worth seeing how, on the run, I pick up a rolling ball. It is easier if the ball is stationary but the basic technique is the same.

My eyes are fixed on the ball as I approach it and I have my hands ready. Just as I reach the ball I bend right down and scoop the ball off the ground with one hand (11/1). In one continuous movement, the hand scoops the ball up into the other hand (11/2 and 11/3).

I scarcely slow down on approaching the ball, and as long as I remain balanced I am able to accelerate away with the ball safely held in two hands (11/3). The faster the ball is moving, the more cautious my approach. It is important to bend right down and place one foot beside the ball. Here, I use my right hand so I put my right foot as close to the ball as possible. My left knee in 11/1 and my right knee in 11/2 come very close to touching the ground.

All through my career I have had to scoop up stray rolling balls from scrum, line-out and loose play, and I practised until I could do it virtually flat out. But to begin with, I suggest you keep the ball stationary and gradually increase the speed at which you approach the ball.

11/2

11/3

Opposite top left: *Ireland's Tony Ward passing during an Irish international and* (top right) *Scotland's Ian McGeechan about to pass.* Below: *John Frame completely commits one of the opposition centres before passing in the match against Hawkes Bay during Scotland's tour of New Zealand in 1975*

# 3 BEATING A MAN

I have never been a great believer in a back division becoming obsessed by dozens of complicated moves. I have always played in sides at both club and national level who have had enough skilful players to score tries from good second-phase possession by their own individual ability. Players like Phil Bennett, Barry John, Gerald Davies, Andy Irvine, Mike Gibson and Dave Duckham are all capable of splitting a defence wide open with good possession from broken play.

Set-piece possession doesn't offer the same scope in attack and, of course, the opposition defence is much better organized and more plentiful from first-phase possession. But I believe set-piece moves by the backs should be limited and kept simple. The idea of these moves should be simply to create an overlap which results in two attackers being faced with only one defender. This can be done most easily by introducing a running full-back into the line from both scrum and line-out. The blind-side wing and even the scrum-half can also be used to create the extra man, and most moves, apart from those merely trying to set up second-phase possession, should be aimed at simply trying to create an extra man. So much of

rugby is geared to creating a situation in which two attackers are left to confront one defender that it is vital the attacking side can always capitalize on this situation. It does not really matter whether this two-against-one situation has come from quick accurate passing and straight running from loose play or a set-piece move involving the full-back or perhaps an outside break by one of the centres. What does matter is that whenever there are two players against one, the attacking side should always score.

I have played in countless matches over the years when this sort of golden opportunity has been squandered and there is really no excuse for it. I can remember bad passes hitting the ground, forward passes ruining the move, good passes being dropped, the player with the ball being tackled before he had managed to pass and, on many occasions, the player passing far too soon and the receiver being tackled.

Yet really it should be so simple. Assuming you learn to pass and handle properly, all you have to do is make sure you totally commit the defender to tackle you while you pass to the extra man. It should be a try every time.

*Wales and British Lions wing J. J. Williams leaving opponents flat-footed (with this side-step) during a Welsh international at Cardiff*

## DRAWING A MAN

It is very important to run in as straight a line as possible to commit the defender. Here Barry John runs parallel to the touch-line with the ball held in both hands (14/1). As he is about to pass he commits the defender, Ian Robertson, by falling away towards the touch-line whilst passing the ball in the other direction towards me (14/2 and 14/3). Running at normal speed, Barry would release the ball about two yards from the defender. By falling away on delivering the pass Barry has totally committed the defender and I am free to run in unchallenged (14/4).

It all looks very simple and, if you have practised all the basic handling skills, it is verv simple.

The timing of the pass is crucial and so is the angle of approach. It is vital for Barry to commit the defender completely. If Barry starts running across the pitch towards me before passing, as so many players in this situation do, then the defender can go across the pitch with Barry. When he passes to me, the defender can continue towards me without changing his direction. Not only could he tackle me, but he could also stop me passing back to Barry because he would be between us.

31

15/1

15/3

## SELLING A DUMMY

Suppose the defender assumes you are going to pass and decides to make tracks for the would-be receiver.

Here I have the ball and am about to pass to Barry (15/1 and 15/2). Just as I am on the point of releasing the ball I see that the defender is not totally committed to tackling me; he is actually setting off towards Barry. In this split second, I realize that if I pass the ball, Barry will be tackled at once (15/3). So I know that by hanging on to the ball – selling a dummy – the defender will be too late to change direction. There is no way he will be able to tackle me (15/4 and 15/5).

15/2

15/4

15/5

## SIDE-STEP

It is much harder for one attacker to beat one defender. I can't think of many single-handed attackers who have got past the likes of J.P.R. Williams. But, on the other hand, not many defenders have stopped Gerald Davies, Irvine or Duckham in full flight. Even with a minimum of space to work in, these players could flash past a defender with a lightning side-step.

Everyone can learn the basic technique of a side-step but, of course, the secret is to do it at speed, time it to perfection and accelerate away.

I can remember on two or three occasions playing against Gerald Davies, facing him in full flight when I knew for certain he was going to try and side-step past me. Yet every time he forced me to lean one way whilst at the same time rapidly changing direction and accelerating away in the other direction without allowing me to lay a finger on him.

In this sequence I approach the defender, Barry John, in a fairly straight line. When I am a couple of yards away I step off my left leg (16/1) and land about three feet to my right (16/2). I have drawn the defender across with me and, while he is off balance and going in the wrong direction, I execute a rapid change of direction by side-stepping to my left and accelerating away (16/3 and 16/4).

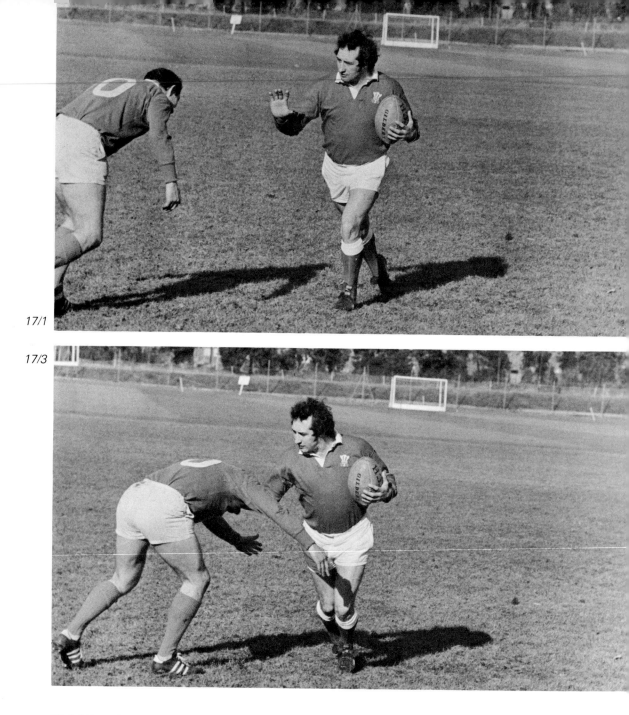

# HAND-OFF

One other method of beating a defender is worth mentioning, and that is the hand-off. It can be used in a very confined space when there is no prospect of side-stepping, passing, selling a dummy or slipping the tackle. It is often used in close-quarter contact when you haven't got up any momentum and you have no way of avoiding the approaching tackler.

As I see the defender, Ian Robertson, approach, I tuck the ball under the arm furthest from him and so free my right hand (17/1). As

the tackler launches himself at me, I drive my right hand into his shoulder with my elbow bent (17/2). (It is quite legal, in fact, to hand off your opponent by pushing aside any part of him – the head, shoulders and arms are the most usual target areas.) As I make contact with his shoulder, I exert maximum downward pressure on the tackler and, at the same time, straighten my right arm to push myself away (17/3). While the defender is abruptly checked, I accelerate away (17/4). I've found over and over again, as I break from the base of the scrum, that a good solid hand-off usually shakes off all but the most resolute of tacklers.

# TACKLING

I have long held the view that the side which tackles better during a match will usually win. When Mike Gibson captained Cambridge University he preached at every training session that a team of fifteen tacklers would beat the world. I accept that philosophy. I'm quite certain that a side made up of fifteen ferocious tacklers will win far more games than they will ever lose.

In the last few seasons, during which Wales have won the Triple Crown a record four times in succession and completed three grand slams, I think far too little has been written about the tremendous defensive qualities the team has shown. Under terrific pressure in several of those recent internationals, we have won all those games as much through our superb defence as for any other reason. Of course it helps to have the greatest tackler in the world at full-back, but J. P. R. Williams can't do it all on his own and the other fourteen have tackled their hearts out in every match. No side in modern rugby can afford to carry a single player who can't tackle and the higher the standard of the match the more important it is. During my twelve years in international rugby I have listened to over fifty team talks by several different Welsh captains, and almost always the final instruction before we leave the changing-room has been to make every tackle count.

Whatever else, don't miss a tackle.

I always loved tackling from the moment I first played rugby and felt that it was an integral part of the game. I often came off the field after a big match in which the real highlight for me had been one vital tackle I'd made.

In the Pontypool–Cardiff Cup match in 1978 I'm sure I got as much satisfaction from one crucial tackle I made in the corner to save a certain try as Gerald Davies got from scoring all four of our tries that afternoon.

What then makes a good tackler? I don't think we could do any better than look at what has made J. P. R. Williams the best in the game. He has unlimited courage – he is absolutely fearless – he is aggressive, totally committed and utterly confident. He relishes tackling because to him every tackle is a personal challenge. Other great players who share his defensive appetite are Fergie McCormick, Mike Gibson and Alastair Hignell.

I think all these players would agree that it is important initially to develop confidence. I'm a great believer in building up that confidence very gradually, and it is essential right away to learn the correct technique. This can then be practised using tackling bags at first and then with a partner – initially at walking pace, and building up to trotting pace, three-quarter speed and finally flat out.

*Two full-backs meet at Twickenham in 1976 as England's Alastair Hignell is tackled just short of the Welsh line by J. P. R. Williams. Despite this crushing tackle, Hignell still manages to make the ball available for the support, although Mervyn Davies tries hard to intercept*

*Welsh flanker Terry Cobner deservedly enjoyed a high reputation as a determined and aggressive tackler. In the first picture he is seen tearing into All Black's flanker Ian Kirkpatrick in the Second Test between the Lions and New Zealand in 1977. On the far page Cobner abruptly halts the progress of England captain Billy Beaumont during the 1977 International at Cardiff*

21/1

21/3

## SIDE-ON TACKLE

Let's start with the easiest type of tackle – bringing someone down from the side. Here former Scotland international Ian Robertson is running with the ball a few yards in from touch, parallel to the touchline.

Once I have lined up my angle of attack, I move towards him at about three-quarter speed so that I can accelerate into the tackle (21/1).

I aim to hit my opponent just below the hips with my left shoulder. My head slips behind the attacker as I wrap my arms tightly around his legs (21/2).

As I accelerate into the tackle, I drive strongly off one leg and that gives me the impetus and power to knock someone over (21/3).

If I go into the tackle fast enough and aggressively enough, I should end up on top of the attacker (21/4).

*21/2*

*21/4*

# TACKLE FROM BEHIND

The tackle from behind is a lot easier than it looks, and has the added bonus of usually looking quite spectacular. As I run behind the attacker my first task is to decide which shoulder to use to tackle him (22/1).

Most players seem to prefer to use their right shoulders, but I believe from an early age everyone should practise tackling with each shoulder so that they become equally proficient with both.

Having decided to use my left shoulder here, I prepare to accelerate into the tackle (22/2).

Again I drive off one leg into the tackle, hitting my opponent with my left shoulder at hip height and at the same time wrapping my arms tightly round his legs (22/3).

I complete the tackle by holding on tightly with my arms and generally pulling him down with my body strength (22/4).

23/1

23/3

# HEAD-ON TACKLE

The head-on tackle demands all the skills used in the other tackles – timing, balance, courage, concentration and determination.

As my opponent comes towards me, I decide which shoulder to use and line my opponent up so that I can hit him with the chosen shoulder in his stomach (23/1).

Having chosen the right shoulder here, again I drive off one leg to hit my opponent in his midriff as I prepare to wrap my arms round his legs (23/2 and 23/3).

By accelerating into the tackle I can knock

my opponent backwards. By clinging firmly to his legs I can make sure he has very little chance of passing one of his team-mates (23/3).

This type of tackle might not work on a charging lock forward. I remember being confronted with a rampaging Colin Meads in New Zealand in 1971 and I let discretion be the better part of valour – with a sixteen-stone monster bearing down on me at speed, it was better to ride the tackle; I allowed Meads almost to run through me, but just as his legs hit my shoulder I clamped my arms round his legs so that he came crashing down on top of me.

47

# KICKING

Every rugby player ought to be able to kick accurately. It is particularly important to learn the correct technique as a youngster because it is very difficult to alter one's style later on. I have played in countless matches at club and even occasionally at international level when a poor front-row forward has made an awful mess of a clearing kick from his own twenty-five, and the opposition have scored. To some extent, it's surprising that so many people kick so badly, because when players turn up for their usual mid-week sessions the first thing they do before .training formally gets under way is to practise their kicking. You can watch school-boys and club players all over the country, prac-tising place-kicking, drop-kicking and punting instead of running up and down the field passing!

Unfortunately, the great majority have never been shown how to kick properly. Without the correct technique they never show any improvement. Under pressure during a match these players make disastrous mistakes.

In this chapter, with the help once again of Barry John, I shall concentrate on the correct technique for every type of kick I ever had to use.

*One of the finest kickers of a ball in recent times, Wales and British Lions fly-half Phil Bennett, kicking for touch during a Test against South Africa in 1974*

25/1     25/2          25/3

# PUNTING

Like golf and cricket the secret of kicking is a delicate combination of balance, timing and fluency. Brute strength is no substitute. With a smooth swing of the leg and my boot meeting the ball at the correct angle, I could kick far further and more accurately than a sixteen-stone forward who just thumped the ball with all the energy he could muster.

Most players hold the ball with the right hand on top at the near end and the left underneath and at the side of the front of the ball. I must admit I use this technique when I'm under pres-sure in the heat of a match and you can see this grip demonstrated later on in the chapter (29/1 and 29/2). But given time and room I usually hold the ball at a slight angle with my right hand underneath and my left hand on top at the side (25/1 and 25/2). It doesn't matter which way you hold the ball as long as you are comfortable and you follow these four basic principles.

Firstly, you must never throw the ball up in the air before kicking it. It should be either dropped straight down on to your boot (25/3) or

25/4                                                            25/5

even pushed downwards.

Secondly, it must land on your boot at exactly the same angle as it leaves your hands (25/3 and 25/4).

Thirdly, as it meets your boot at that angle, your foot should be pointing away from you (25/4).

Lastly, you should finish with a good high follow-through (25/5).

I have already mentioned the importance of balance and here I have just taken one step forward before kicking. My eyes are on the ball the whole time and my weight is on my left leg. The faster the kicker is moving, the harder it becomes to be perfectly balanced and the more difficult it is to kick.

Another fault is to try to kick the ball too far. The ball should be stroked and not simply belted as hard as possible. Barry John and Phil Bennett were the best punters of a ball I played with, closely followed by Bob Hiller and Tom Kiernan. These four could all kick further and more accurately than any forward giant who relied on brute strength.

26/1          26/2          26/3

# KICKING WITH THE LEFT FOOT

The same rules apply for the left foot – usually the weaker – and if you start to practise with it from the very start, there is no reason why you should not reach an equally high standard with both feet. It all helps to make a player a more complete footballer, and everyone who can be bothered to practise regularly can become a good kicker.

I began practising my kicking when I was about ten or eleven and I used to play a game called 'gaining ground' against one of my friends. Whenever we had some free time we would play one against one for hours every week kicking to touch. Where the ball went into touch, the next player would come back into play five yards and then kick back to touch. And so on for ages, sometimes using the right leg and sometimes making the left leg compulsory for half an hour. If my opponent missed touch, I could advance twenty yards from where the ball landed. I learned from a very early age the crucial importance of accuracy. It is always better to find a twenty-five-yard touch than to kick sixty yards and miss touch.

Above, keeping my eyes on the ball, I drop it at an angle on to my pointed foot and, with my weight on my right foot, I finish with a high follow-through.

*Putting all the basic rules into practice, Barry John, head down and perfectly balanced, kicks to touch during the 1972 international against France at Cardiff*

29/1    29/2

# KICKING FROM THE BASE OF A SCRUM

As a scrum-half I have found it necessary during the latter part of my career to develop two rather specialized forms of punting which I've used to great effect to keep my side going forward, even when the pack and myself have been under great pressure. One is used from a scrum and the other from a line-out.

Let's take the scrum first. Here, my side have won a scrum and, from a good channelled heel or even scrappy untidy possession, I reckon I can get a punishing kick from the narrowest of angles to push my side down the touchline.

After putting the ball into the scrum, I scurry round for the heel ready to scoop the ball up and kick in one movement.

I must act very quickly indeed or I could either be tackled by my opposite number or have the kick charged down by the opposition back-row. Keeping low to the ground I pick the ball up as soon as it emerges from the scrum (29/1).

In almost the same movement I prepare to kick by straightening up just enough to give myself room to get in the kick (29/2).

I push the ball on to my boot after only a very

29/3    29/4

short backswing (29/3), and I have a restricted follow-through (29/4).

Throughout this kick, I am crouching low to the ground and my kicking leg whips quickly through, striking the ball with a stabbing, punching movement.

Before the scrum goes down, I always check the target area so I know exactly where I'm aiming and don't have to waste any time once the ball has been heeled. It is essential that I have this mental picture in my mind before I put the ball into the scrum, as I may well not have a chance to survey the scene, even briefly, once the ball is out, if it is an untidy heel or the opposition are quick to break.

I developed this type of kick on the British Lions tour of South Africa in 1974 where it was particularly effective on the hard grounds.

It takes a lot of hard practice to develop the art of kicking the ball from an unnatural crouching position so that it bounces at least once before rolling into touch. But I believe it is well worth all the practice – as I think I have proved, it is a very easy way to gain forty yards.

# KICKING FROM A LINE-OUT

From a line-out, a scrum-half can relieve pressure in defence, or put pressure on the opposition in attack, by hoisting a towering punt over the forwards. This tactic should not be overdone, but it creates a useful variation if used very occasionally.

Barry John is seen here winning good line-out possession (30/1)!

While the ball is in the air I prepare to catch and kick in one movement, if possible, to avoid the risk of the ball being charged down, and right away I am side-on to the opposition (30/2).

Taking one step away from the line-out, if necessary, I now turn my back to the opposition and prepare to hoist the ball over the forwards (30/3).

Without wasting any time I hook the ball over the two packs, either into touch if I'm in deep defence or high into the box if my side are on the attack (30/4).

To help me find the height I need, I must have a high follow-through (30/5).

Obviously speed of action is essential for success. The ball must travel from the line-out jumper's hand to my boot as quickly as possible.

30/4       30/5

# THE DROP-KICK

Although half-backs and full-backs probably drop more goals than the other twelve members of each team added together, I have seen some amazing sights during my career which I would never have believed possible. I've played in matches where a front-row forward has dropped a goal, and I can even remember one lock-forward once winning a match with a drop goal!

But with great respect to the Bobby Windsors and Alan Martins of this world, I have chosen one of the great drop-goal experts of recent years, Barry John, to demonstrate the technique.

For the right-footed drop-kick the ball is held with one hand down each side and slightly leaning towards the kicker (31/1). As in the punt, the ball must not be thrown up in the air but dropped straight on the ground (31/2). With his full weight on his left leg and left foot slightly behind the ball, Barry swings smoothly through to strike the ball just as it hits the ground (31/3). The ball should land on its end, leaning, as it does here, towards the kicker (31/3). Still perfectly balanced on his left leg, Barry finishes with a smooth, straight follow-through (31/4). Note how at each stage Barry has his head over the ball and his eyes fixed on it.

32/1    32/2

## PLACE-KICKING

Place-kicking is a bit like putting on the golf course – there are days when everything goes right and there are days when nothing seems to go right. No one can guarantee success but, if, like Barry John and Phil Bennett, your technique is good, then the odds are at least in your favour. Of the three different styles in common use, let's look first at the straight-on kick.

First of all it is important to line the ball up accurately. Barry has made a small hole for the ball and has placed it absolutely vertically with the lace facing the posts (32/1).

He then addresses the ball with his left foot 3 or 4 inches behind and 3 or 4 inches to the side of it. That is exactly where his left foot should land when he kicks it (32/2).

After a good look at the posts he takes about half a dozen paces back, has a final look at the posts and then concentrates on the ball (32/3).

With his eyes fixed on the ball he begins a rhythmic approach (32/4).

32/4

His left foot lands just behind and to the side of the ball and supports his full weight. With his eyes still on the ball, his right leg swings smoothly through (32/5).

Still balanced on his left leg, Barry finishes by

32/3

32/5

32/6

following through in a straight line (32/6).

Barry maintains that the most important single element in determining whether someone is a good or bad place-kicker is the position of his non-kicking foot as he is about to strike the ball. Make sure you concentrate on that non-kicking foot in practice.

Be sure to finish with a good straight follow-through and, as in punting, keep your head over the ball until you've actually kicked it.

33/1

33/3

# THE TORPEDO KICK

This type of kick is not so popular nowadays, but Wales have been very grateful during the last few years to Allan Martin, who has kicked some prodigious goals using the torpedo kick.

This time the ball is placed on the ground so that it is pointing toward the posts. It is usually used only for long-range kicks as it is not as accurate as the other two methods, but a torpedo kick can carry enormous distances.

With his back to the posts Barry has dug quite a deep hole with his heel. He then puts the ball in the hole so that the ball is facing the posts (33/1).

The important non-kicking foot lands just short of the ball with the head and eyes on the ball (33/2).

The approach to the ball is dead straight and so too is the follow-through (33/3 and 33/4).

33/2

33/4

63

34/1  34/2                                    34/3

# 'ROUND-THE-CORNER' PLACE-KICKING

This style has become increasingly popular in recent years and has been used to great advantage by Barry, Phil Bennett, Andy Irvine and Tony Ward.

Once the ball has been lined up, Barry retires at an angle so that he will approach the ball round the corner like a soccer player (34/1).

Head down and eyes on the ball, Barry takes about six strides to the ball.

As always, the non-kicking foot is crucial. This time it lands level with the ball and about six inches to the left. This leg takes all Barry's weight (34/2).

Perfectly balanced, Barry follows through slightly across in front of his body (34/3).

Whichever style you decide to adopt, first perfect the technique and then practise regularly at every training session. To gain confidence you should begin with simple kicks from in front of the posts and gradually add to the distance and angle. As with everything else, practice makes perfect.